Fredrick Wonders

How To Get Millions Of Subscribers On YouTube

Proven Strategies and Insider Secrets for Skyrocketing Your Channel's Growth

First published by Fredrick Wonders 2024

Copyright © 2024 by Fredrick Wonders

All rights reserved. No part of this publication may be reproduced, stored or transmitted in any form or by any means, electronic, mechanical, photocopying, recording, scanning, or otherwise without written permission from the publisher. It is illegal to copy this book, post it to a website, or distribute it by any other means without permission.

First edition

This book was professionally typeset on Reedsy
Find out more at reedsy.com

Dedication

To all the creators who dare to dream big and share their unique voices with the world. This book is for you.

Fredrick Wonders

Epigraph

"The journey of a thousand miles begins with a single step."
— Lao Tzu

Fredrick					Wonders

Contents

Foreword 1
Preface 4
Acknowledgement 7
1. Laying the Foundation 10
2. Crafting Quality Content 14
3. Building Your Brand 19
4. Mastering SEO and Metadata 25
5. Engaging with Your Audience 32
6. Collaborations and Networking 39
7. Monetization Strategies 47
8. Leveraging Analytics and Insights 55
9. Building a Strong Brand Identity 64
10. Scaling and Sustaining Growth 72
    1.
    2.
    3.
    4.
    5.
    6.
    7.
    8.

9.
10.
11.
12.

Foreword

Foreword

In the digital age, YouTube has become much more than a platform for sharing videos. It has transformed into a dynamic ecosystem where creativity, entrepreneurship, and community converge. For many, YouTube is a stage where dreams are born and careers are made. It is a place where anyone, from anywhere, can reach millions of people around the world.

I've had the privilege of witnessing the rise of countless YouTube stars—individuals who started with nothing more than a camera and an idea, and who have gone on to amass millions of subscribers and build incredible communities. The journey to achieving such success is fascinating, filled with moments of triumph and learning. But one thing is clear: behind every successful YouTube channel is a strategy, a relentless passion, and a deep understanding of what makes content resonate.

"How to Get Millions of Subscribers on YouTube" is an invaluable resource for anyone serious about scaling their YouTube presence. This book is a testament to the fact that with the right approach, dedication, and a little bit of guidance, anyone can turn their YouTube aspirations into reality.

The author has meticulously broken down the process into clear, actionable steps that demystify the path to YouTube success. From identifying your unique niche and creating captivating content to leveraging SEO and engaging with your audience, every chapter is packed with insights that can help you grow and sustain a massive following. What makes this book particularly special is its focus on authenticity and the importance of building a genuine connection with your audience—principles that are at the heart of every successful channel.

As you dive into this book, you'll discover the tools and strategies that top YouTubers use to build their empires. You'll learn how to navigate the ever-evolving landscape of YouTube, stay ahead of trends, and continuously innovate your content. But beyond the tactics and techniques, this book will inspire you to stay true to your vision, embrace your unique voice, and enjoy every step of your YouTube journey.

I am excited for you to embark on this transformative adventure. Whether you're starting from scratch or looking to elevate your existing channel, the insights and advice in these pages will equip you with the knowledge and confidence to reach millions of subscribers. Remember, the sky is the limit on YouTube, and with this book as your guide, you are well on your way to achieving greatness.

Here's to your success and the incredible journey ahead!

[Fredrick Wonders]

Preface

Preface

Welcome to "How to Get Millions of Subscribers on YouTube." If you're holding this book, chances are you have a dream of turning your passion for creating videos into a thriving YouTube channel with millions of subscribers. You might be wondering if it's truly possible to achieve such monumental success in a sea of countless creators. The answer is a resounding yes—and this book will show you how.

I remember the days when YouTube was just a platform for sharing random clips and funny videos. It has since evolved into a global powerhouse where careers are made, businesses are built, and dreams are realized. The journey to YouTube stardom is thrilling, but it's also filled with challenges, strategic decisions, and a lot of hard work. However, with the right guidance and mindset, you can navigate these waters successfully and achieve the extraordinary.

In this book, you'll find a comprehensive roadmap that takes you from zero to millions of subscribers. We'll delve into every aspect of YouTube growth, from identifying your niche and creating captivating content to mastering SEO, engaging your audience, and leveraging analytics. You'll learn the secrets behind building a strong brand identity, diversifying your revenue streams, and staying ahead of trends in a rapidly changing landscape.

This isn't just a collection of tips and tricks. It's a deep dive into the strategies that top YouTubers use to grow their channels. You'll gain insights from real-world examples, actionable advice, and expert knowledge that I've gathered from studying and working with some of the most successful creators on the platform.

As you embark on this journey, remember that success on YouTube is not about quick fixes or viral hits. It's about consistency, authenticity, and understanding your audience. It's about creating content that you're passionate about and that resonates with others. And most importantly, it's about enjoying the process and celebrating every milestone along the way.

So, whether you're a complete beginner or an experienced creator looking to take your channel to the next level, this book is for you. Prepare to unlock the secrets to YouTube stardom and transform your channel into a thriving community with millions of loyal subscribers.

Let's get started!

[Fredrick   Wonders]

Acknowledgement

Acknowledgements

Creating "How to Get Millions of Subscribers on YouTube" has been an incredible journey, and it wouldn't have been possible without the support, insights, and encouragement of many individuals. I am deeply grateful to everyone who contributed to this project.

First and foremost, I want to thank the countless YouTube creators who have inspired me with their creativity, perseverance, and passion. Your stories of growth and success have been the cornerstone of this book, and I am honored to share the strategies and lessons you've generously imparted.

A heartfelt thank you to my family and friends for their unwavering support and belief in this project. Your encouragement has been my driving force, and your patience during the countless hours spent writing and researching has been invaluable.

To my mentors and colleagues in the digital media and content creation industry, thank you for your guidance and for sharing your wealth of knowledge. Your insights have enriched this book and provided a deeper understanding of what it takes to succeed on YouTube.

I am also grateful to the dedicated team of editors, designers, and publishers who worked tirelessly to bring this book to life. Your expertise and attention to detail have ensured that every aspect of this book is polished and professional.

A special thanks to the beta readers and early reviewers who provided feedback and helped shape the final version of this book. Your constructive criticism and suggestions have been instrumental in making this book the best it can be.

Finally, I want to express my appreciation to you, the reader. Your passion for creating and sharing content is what makes YouTube such an extraordinary platform. I hope this book serves as a valuable resource on your journey to achieving millions of subscribers and beyond.

Thank you all for being a part of this journey. Your contributions and support have made this book a reality, and for that, I am forever grateful.

Fredrick   Wonders

1

Laying the Foundation

Laying the Foundation

Introduction to YouTube

Understanding the Platform: YouTube is more than just a video-sharing site; it's a dynamic ecosystem where content creators and audiences interact. Learn about the history of YouTube, its growth, and its importance in the digital age.

The Algorithm: The YouTube algorithm plays a critical role in determining which videos get recommended to viewers. Explore how the algorithm works, including factors like watch time, click-through rate (CTR), and viewer engagement.

Potential: YouTube's vast user base offers unparalleled potential for reaching millions. Understand the diverse audience and the opportunities it presents for various niches.

Setting Goals

Identifying Your Niche: Your niche is the specific area you focus on, such as gaming, beauty, education, or tech reviews. Choosing a niche helps target a specific audience and stand out in the crowded YouTube landscape.

Target Audience: Define your target audience by considering age, interests, and demographics. Knowing who you're creating for will guide your content creation and marketing strategies.

SMART Goals: Establish Specific, Measurable, Achievable, Relevant, and Time-bound goals. For example, "Gain 10,000 subscribers in six months" is a clear and actionable goal.

Creating a Business Plan content Strategy: Develop a content plan outlining the type of videos you'll create, their frequency, and the themes you'll cover. Consider a mix of evergreen content (timeless) and trending topics to attract new viewers and retain existing ones.

Schedule: Consistency is key on YouTube. Create a realistic posting schedule (e.g., once a week) and stick to it. This helps build a loyal audience who knows when to expect new content.

Milestones: Break down your long-term goals into smaller milestones. Celebrate achievements like reaching 100, 1,000, and 10,000 subscribers to stay motivated and track progress.

Budgeting: Outline a budget for equipment, software, marketing, and other expenses. Starting with minimal investment is possible, but knowing when to upgrade can help improve your content quality.

The Mindset for Success

Patience and Persistence: Building a successful YouTube channel takes time and effort. Be prepared for slow growth initially and remain persistent.

Adaptability: The digital landscape changes rapidly. Stay flexible and be ready to adapt your content and strategies based on analytics and feedback.

Passion and Authenticity: Your enthusiasm for your niche will shine through in your videos. Authenticity builds trust and helps form a genuine connection with your audience.

By laying a solid foundation, you set the stage for long-term success on YouTube. This chapter prepares you to understand the platform, define your goals, and develop a strategic plan to start your journey toward gaining millions of subscribers.

2

Crafting Quality Content

Crafting Quality Content

Content Creation Basics

Essential Equipment: Start with the basics – a decent camera (even a smartphone can work initially), a microphone for clear audio, and proper lighting. As your channel grows, consider upgrading to more professional equipment.

Software Tools: Familiarize yourself with video editing software like Adobe Premiere Pro, Final Cut Pro, or free options like DaVinci Resolve and Shotcut. Learn basic editing skills to enhance your video quality.

Content Planning: Plan your videos in advance. Create an outline or script to ensure your videos have a clear structure and flow. This helps maintain viewer interest and ensures you cover all necessary points.

Storytelling

Engaging Introductions: Hook your viewers within the first few seconds. Introduce the topic clearly and explain why it's relevant or exciting.

Narrative Arc: Every video should have a beginning, middle, and end. Introduce the topic, delve into the details, and conclude with a summary or call to action.

Personal Touch: Share personal anecdotes or experiences related to the topic. This makes your content relatable and helps viewers connect with you on a personal level.

Production Tips

Lighting: Good lighting is crucial. Natural light works well, but you can also use ring lights or softbox lights for better illumination. Ensure your face and key areas are well-lit to maintain a professional look.

Sound: Clear audio is vital. Use an external microphone for better sound quality. Avoid recording in noisy environments and consider using a pop filter to minimize background noise.

Editing: Effective editing enhances viewer experience. Use cuts to maintain a fast pace, add text overlays for emphasis, and include background music to set the tone. Avoid over-editing, which can distract from the content.

Content Formats and Variety

Different Formats: Experiment with various formats like tutorials, reviews, vlogs, interviews, and live streams. This keeps your content fresh and caters to different viewer preferences.

Series and Playlists: Create series or playlists around specific topics. This encourages binge-watching and helps retain viewers on your channel for longer periods.

Challenges and Trends: Participate in popular challenges or trends within your niche. This can boost your visibility and attract new viewers who are searching for trending content.

Thumbnail and Title Optimization

Eye-Catching Thumbnails: Design custom thumbnails that grab attention. Use high-quality images, bold text, and vibrant colors. Ensure the thumbnail accurately represents the video content.

Compelling Titles: Craft titles that are both informative and intriguing. Incorporate keywords for better searchability but avoid clickbait, as it can harm your credibility and viewer trust.

Creating Value

Educational Content: Offer informative and valuable content that teaches viewers something new. How-to videos, tutorials, and guides are popular formats for educational content.

Entertainment: Ensure your videos are enjoyable to watch. Inject humor, use dynamic visuals, and maintain a lively pace to keep viewers entertained.

Inspiration and Motivation: Share inspiring stories or motivational messages. Positive content that resonates emotionally with viewers can drive engagement and shares.

Feedback and Improvement

Viewer Feedback: Pay attention to viewer comments and feedback. Use constructive criticism to improve your content and address any issues.

Analytics: Regularly review your video performance using YouTube Analytics. Analyze metrics like watch time, audience retention, and click-through rate to understand what's working and what needs improvement.

Continuous Learning: Stay updated with the latest trends, techniques, and tools in video production and content creation. Invest time in learning and refining your skills to keep your content top-notch.

By mastering the art of content creation, you'll be able to produce high-quality, engaging videos that attract and retain viewers, setting the stage for substantial growth on YouTube.

3

Building Your Brand

Building Your Brand

Visual Identity

Thumbnails: Thumbnails are your video's first impression. Create custom thumbnails with a consistent style. Use bright colors, bold text, and clear images to stand out. Ensure they are visually appealing and accurately represent the content.

Channel Art: Design an attractive banner that encapsulates your brand. It should reflect your channel's theme and include your upload schedule if possible.

Logos and Watermarks: Develop a unique logo for your channel. Use it as a watermark on your videos to build brand recognition and deter content theft.

Consistency

Visual Consistency: Maintain a consistent color scheme, font style, and overall aesthetic across your thumbnails, channel art, and video graphics. This makes your content instantly recognizable.

Content Consistency: Stick to a regular posting schedule. Whether it's daily, weekly, or bi-weekly, consistency helps build anticipation and reliability with your audience.

Brand Voice: Develop a consistent tone and style in your videos. Whether it's humorous, educational, or inspirational, a consistent voice helps viewers connect with your brand.

Authenticity

Be Genuine: Authenticity fosters trust and loyalty. Share your true self, including your successes and struggles. Viewers appreciate transparency and honesty.

Connect Personally: Use personal anecdotes and speak directly to your audience. Make them feel like part of a community.

Avoid Over-Production: While high-quality production is important, overly polished videos can sometimes feel impersonal. Balance professionalism with a touch of raw, real moments.

Developing a Unique Value Proposition (UVP)

Identify Your UVP: Determine what makes your channel unique. It could be your perspective, style, niche, or personality.

Communicate Your UVP: Clearly convey your UVP in your channel trailer, about section, and across social media platforms. Let viewers know what they can expect and why they should subscribe.

Channel Trailer and About Section

Channel Trailer: Create a short, engaging trailer that introduces new visitors to your channel. Highlight your best content and your channel's purpose.

About Section: Write a compelling description in your channel's about section. Include your UVP, upload schedule, and a call to action encouraging visitors to subscribe.

Engagement and Interaction

Encourage Comments: Prompt viewers to leave comments by asking questions or requesting feedback. Respond to comments to build a sense of community.

Live Streams: Host live streams to interact with your audience in real-time. This fosters a deeper connection and allows for immediate engagement.

Polls and Surveys: Use YouTube's community tab to post polls and surveys. This helps you understand your audience's preferences and makes them feel involved in your content creation process.

Utilizing Social Media

Cross-Promotion: Share your videos on social media platforms like Instagram, Twitter, Facebook, and TikTok. Each platform has unique features that can help you reach different segments of your audience.

Behind-the-Scenes Content: Share behind-the-scenes photos and stories on social media. This provides additional content and deepens the connection with your audience.

Engage and Grow: Actively engage with followers on social media. Respond to comments, share user-generated content, and participate in relevant conversations.

Building a Community

Foster Loyalty: Create a sense of belonging by giving your audience a name, recognizing loyal fans, and creating exclusive content for them.

User-Generated Content: Encourage viewers to create and share content related to your channel. Feature their content in your videos or social media to show appreciation and strengthen community bonds.

Collaborative Projects: Involve your audience in collaborative projects or challenges. This increases engagement and makes viewers feel like they are a part of your creative process.

Consistency in Quality and Content

Quality Control: Regularly assess and maintain the quality of your videos. Invest in better equipment and editing software as your channel grows.

Evolving Content: While consistency is important, don't be afraid to innovate. Introduce new series or formats to keep your content fresh and exciting.

By building a strong, authentic brand, you create a loyal community around your channel, which is essential for long-term growth and success on YouTube.

4

Mastering SEO and Metadata

Mastering SEO and Metadata

Keyword Research

Importance of Keywords: Keywords help YouTube understand the content of your videos and match them with relevant searches. Proper keyword usage can significantly increase your video's discoverability.

Tools for Keyword Research: Use tools like Google Trends, TubeBuddy, VidIQ, and Keyword Tool to find popular and relevant keywords in your niche.

Identifying Keywords: Look for keywords with a good balance of search volume and competition. Long-tail keywords (phrases of 3-5 words) are often less competitive and more specific.

Optimizing Titles and Description

Crafting Effective Titles: Your title should be compelling and include your main keyword. Aim for clarity and curiosity. Titles should be between 50-70 characters to avoid being cut off.

Examples: "How to Start a Successful YouTube Channel in 2024" or "Top 10 Tips for Beginner YouTubers"

Writing Descriptions: The description box is an opportunity to provide context and additional information.

Keyword Integration: Naturally incorporate your main and related keywords in the first few lines of the description.

Structure: Use the first 100-150 characters to summarize your video. Include links to related videos, timestamps, and relevant social media or website links.

Call to Action (CTA): Encourage viewers to like, comment, and subscribe.

Tags and Hashtags

Tags: Tags help YouTube understand your video's content and context. Use a mix of broad and specific tags related to your video.

Example: For a video about "baking chocolate chip cookies," use tags like "baking," "chocolate chip cookies recipe," "easy baking recipes," and "cookie tutorials."

Hashtags: Use relevant hashtags in your description or title to improve discoverability. Hashtags should be specific to the content and relevant trends.

Example: #BakingTips #ChocolateChipCookies #EasyRecipes

Thumbnails

Designing Thumbnails: Thumbnails should be eye-catching and relevant to the video content. Use high-quality images, bold text, and contrasting colors.

Consistency: Maintain a consistent style across your thumbnails to build brand recognition.

Best Practices: Include your face in the thumbnail if possible, as viewers are drawn to human expressions. Ensure text is readable even in small sizes.

Closed Captions and Transcripts

Importance of Captions: Closed captions improve accessibility and can boost your SEO. They help YouTube understand your video content better.

Adding Captions: You can use YouTube's automatic captions as a base and then edit for accuracy. Alternatively, you can upload your own captions file.

Transcripts: Including a transcript in the video description or as a pinned comment can also enhance SEO and provide value to viewers.

End Screens and Cards

End Screens: Use the last 20 seconds of your video to promote other content, encourage subscriptions, and include CTAs.

Elements: Add elements like links to other videos, playlists, subscribe buttons, or external websites.

Best Practices: Ensure your end screen is visually appealing and does not obstruct the main content.

Cards: Use cards to link to other videos, playlists, channels, or external sites during the video. They appear as small pop-ups and can be strategically placed to retain viewer interest.

Playlists

Creating Playlists: Organize your videos into playlists to make it easier for viewers to find related content. This encourages binge-watching and increases watch time.

Keyword Optimization: Include keywords in playlist titles and descriptions.

Promote Playlists: Mention relevant playlists in your videos and link to them in descriptions and cards.

Engagement and Retention

Audience Retention: Aim to keep viewers watching your videos as long as possible. High retention rates signal to YouTube that your content is valuable.

Hook Viewers: Start your video with a strong hook to keep viewers engaged from the beginning.

Pacing: Maintain a good pace to keep viewers interested. Avoid long pauses or unnecessary filler.

Encouraging Interaction: Prompt viewers to like, comment, and subscribe. Engagement signals help improve your video's ranking.

Questions: Ask questions or solicit opinions to encourage comments.

Likes and Shares: Politely ask viewers to like and share if they enjoyed the content.

Regular Analysis and Adaptation

YouTube Analytics: Regularly review your analytics to understand what's working and what isn't. Focus on metrics like watch time, CTR, audience retention, and engagement.

CTR (Click-Through Rate): Measure how often viewers click on your video after seeing the thumbnail and title.

Watch Time: Total amount of time viewers spend watching your videos.

Audience Retention: Percentage of the video watched by viewers.

A/B Testing: Experiment with different titles, thumbnails, and descriptions to see what resonates best with your audience.

Adapt and Improve: Use insights from your analytics to refine your SEO strategies and content creation process.

By mastering SEO and optimizing your metadata, you can significantly improve your video's discoverability, attract more viewers, and grow your subscriber base.

5

Engaging with Your Audience

Engaging with Your Audience

Community Building

Creating a Sense of Belonging: Foster a welcoming environment where viewers feel like part of a community. Use inclusive language and address your audience directly.

Naming Your Audience: Give your audience a name that reflects your brand and creates a sense of identity.

Exclusive Content: Offer exclusive content or perks to loyal subscribers, such as behind-the-scenes footage, early access to videos, or special shoutouts.

Interaction Strategies

Responding to Comments: Engage with viewers by responding to comments on your videos. Acknowledge positive feedback, answer questions, and address constructive criticism.

Pinned Comments: Use pinned comments to highlight important messages or questions and prompt further discussion.

Top Commenter Recognition: Regularly recognize and appreciate top commenters to encourage more engagement.

Live Streaming: Host live streams to interact with your audience in real time. This builds stronger connections and allows for immediate feedback.

Q&A Sessions: Hold Q&A sessions during live streams to answer viewer questions and discuss topics of interest.

Live Events: Organize live events around special occasions, milestones, or new content releases.

Community Tab: Utilize the YouTube Community tab to post updates, polls, and behind-the-scenes content. This keeps your audience engaged between video uploads.

Polls and Surveys: Conduct polls to understand viewer preferences and involve them in content decisions.

Teasers and Sneak Peeks: Share teasers and sneak peeks of upcoming videos to build anticipation.

Utilizing Social Media

Cross-Promotion: Share your videos on social media platforms like Instagram, Twitter, Facebook, and TikTok. Tailor your content to each platform's unique features and audience.

Consistent Posting: Maintain a consistent posting schedule across social media to stay top of mind with your audience.

Engaging Content: Post a mix of content, including video clips, behind-the-scenes photos, stories, and updates.

Building a Presence: Actively engage with followers on social media. Respond to comments, share user-generated content, and participate in relevant conversations.

Hashtags: Use relevant hashtags to increase visibility and reach new audiences.

ollaborations: Collaborate with influencers or other content creators on social media to expand your reach.

Audience Feedback and Improvement

Soliciting Feedback: Encourage viewers to provide feedback on your videos. Ask them what they liked, what could be improved, and what they want to see in future content.

Surveys and Forms: Use surveys or feedback forms to gather detailed input from your audience.

Comment Analysis: Regularly review comments to identify common themes and areas for improvement.

Implementing Feedback: Use audience feedback to improve your content and address viewer preferences. Communicate any changes or updates based on their input.

Acknowledging Feedback: Show appreciation for viewer feedback by mentioning it in your videos and explaining how it influenced your content.

Creating Interactive Content

Challenges and Contests: Host challenges or contests that encourage viewer participation. Offer prizes or shoutouts to winners.

User-Generated Content: Invite viewers to create and share content related to your channel. Feature their submissions in your videos or on social media.

Interactive Videos: Create interactive videos with elements like polls, quizzes, or choose-your-own-adventure formats to engage viewers actively.

Calls to Action (CTAs): Use clear and compelling CTAs in your videos to guide viewer actions.

Subscribe: Encourage viewers to subscribe to your channel and turn on notifications.

Like and Comment: Ask viewers to like and comment on your videos to boost engagement.

Share: Prompt viewers to share your videos with friends and on social media.

Engagement Analytics

Monitoring Engagement: Use YouTube Analytics to track engagement metrics such as likes, comments, shares, and watch time.

Engagement Rate: Calculate your engagement rate by dividing the total number of engagements (likes, comments, shares) by the total number of views.

Identifying Trends: Analyze trends in viewer engagement to understand what types of content resonate most with your audience.

Adjusting Strategies: Use engagement data to refine your content and interaction strategies. Focus on producing more of what your audience loves and less of what they don't.

Experimentation: Experiment with different content formats, interaction methods, and CTAs to find what works best for your channel.

Continuous Improvement: Regularly review and adjust your strategies based on engagement metrics and audience feedback.

By effectively engaging with your audience, you build a loyal and active community around your channel. This not only increases viewer retention and satisfaction but also encourages organic growth through word-of-mouth and social sharing.

6

Collaborations and Networking

Collaborations and Networking

Finding Collaborators

Identifying Potential Collaborators: Look for other YouTubers or influencers within your niche or related fields. Focus on those with similar audience sizes and engagement levels to ensure a mutually beneficial collaboration.

Research: Watch their content to understand their style, audience, and values. Ensure they align with your brand and goals.

Social Media: Utilize platforms like Twitter, Instagram, and LinkedIn to find and connect with potential collaborators.

Collaboration Platforms: Use platforms like CollabSpace, Grapevine, or FameBit to discover and connect with potential collaborators.

Approaching Collaborators

Crafting Your Pitch: Create a personalized and professional pitch when reaching out to potential collaborators.

Introduction: Introduce yourself and your channel briefly.

Purpose: Explain why you want to collaborate and what you hope to achieve.

Proposal: Outline your collaboration idea, including the type of content, format, and how it will benefit both parties.

Value Proposition: Highlight the mutual benefits, such as cross-promotion and audience growth.

Building Relationships: Foster genuine relationships with potential collaborators before proposing a collaboration.

Engage with Their Content: Comment on their videos, share their content, and participate in their live streams or social media discussions.

Networking Events: Attend industry events, workshops, and YouTube conventions to meet and connect with other creators in person.

Collaboration Ideas

Joint Videos: Create videos together, either in person or virtually, where you both contribute to the content.

Guest Appearances: Feature each other in your videos to introduce your audiences to each other's channels.

Challenges: Participate in popular challenges or create your own challenge for both audiences to engage with.

Shoutouts and Mentions: Give shoutouts to each other in your videos, descriptions, and social media posts to direct your audiences to your collaborator's channel.

Series or Playlists: Develop a series or playlist together where each episode is hosted on alternating channels. This encourages viewers to visit both channels.

Interviews and Q&A: Conduct interviews or Q&A sessions with each other to provide valuable content and insights to your audiences.

Contests and Giveaways: Host contests or giveaways together, encouraging viewers to subscribe to both channels to participate.

Maximizing Collaboration Impact

Promotion: Actively promote the collaboration on all your social media platforms and encourage your collaborator to do the same.

Teasers and Announcements: Share teasers and announcements leading up to the collaboration to build anticipation.

Cross-Promotion: Use social media posts, stories, and live sessions to promote the collaboration before and after its release.

Consistency: Plan a series of collaborations over time rather than one-off projects. Consistent collaborations build stronger relationships and sustained audience growth.

Engagement: Actively engage with comments and feedback on collaboration videos. Show appreciation to new viewers and encourage them to subscribe.

Networking Events

YouTube Conventions and Conferences: Attend events like VidCon, Playlist Live, and YouTube Creator Summit to network with other creators, learn from industry experts, and gain inspiration.

Workshops and Panels: Participate in workshops and panel discussions to gain insights and connect with other attendees.

Meetups and Socials: Attend informal meetups and social events to build relationships in a relaxed setting.

Online Communities and Forums: Join online communities, forums, and groups related to YouTube and your niche.

Reddit: Participate in relevant subreddits like r/YouTubers and r/NewTubers to share experiences, seek advice, and find collaboration opportunities.

Facebook Groups: Join and engage with Facebook groups focused on YouTube creators and your specific niche.

Networking Etiquette: Practice good networking etiquette by being respectful, genuine, and offering value to others.

Follow-Up: After meeting potential collaborators or networking contacts, follow up with a thank-you message and a proposal for future collaboration.

Maintain Relationships: Keep in touch with your network regularly, share their content, and support their projects.

Leveraging Collaborations for Growth

Analyzing Performance: Use YouTube Analytics to measure the success of your collaborations.

Viewership and Engagement: Track changes in viewership, watch time, and engagement metrics for collaboration videos.

Subscriber Growth: Monitor subscriber growth and retention rates following a collaboration.

Refining Strategies: Use insights from your analytics to refine your collaboration strategies.

Successful Formats: Identify which collaboration formats and topics resonate most with your audience.

Improvements: Make improvements based on feedback and performance data to enhance future collaborations.

Scaling Collaborations: As your channel grows, seek opportunities to collaborate with larger creators and brands.

Building Credibility: Successful collaborations build your credibility and make you more attractive to potential collaborators.

Expanding Reach: Collaborate with creators from different niches or industries to expand your reach and attract diverse audiences.

By effectively collaborating and networking, you can significantly boost your channel's visibility, attract new subscribers, and build valuable relationships within the YouTube community.

7

Monetization Strategies

Monetization Strategies

YouTube Partner Program (YPP)

Eligibility Requirements: To join the YouTube Partner Program, your channel must meet specific criteria:

1,000 Subscribers: You need at least 1,000 subscribers.

4,000 Watch Hours: Your videos must have accumulated 4,000 watch hours in the past 12 months.

AdSense Account: You must have an active and approved AdSense account.

Application Process: Once eligible, apply for the YouTube Partner Program through your YouTube Studio dashboard. Follow the guidelines and terms of service.

Ad Revenue: After joining, you can earn money from ads displayed on your videos. Different types of ads include display ads, overlay ads, skippable video ads, and non-skippable video ads.

Ad Formats and Revenue Optimization

Ad Formats: Familiarize yourself with the various ad formats to understand their impact and revenue potential.

Skippable Video Ads: Viewers can skip these ads after 5 seconds. Revenue is earned when viewers watch the ad or click on it.

Non-Skippable Video Ads: These ads must be watched before the video. They are typically shorter and generate higher revenue.

Overlay Ads: Semi-transparent ads that appear on the lower part of the video. They are less intrusive but can generate additional income.

Display Ads: These ads appear next to the video on desktop and are not interruptive.

Increasing Ad Revenue: Implement strategies to maximize ad revenue.

Longer Videos: Videos longer than 8 minutes can have multiple ad breaks, increasing ad revenue potential.

High CPM Niches: Create content in niches with higher Cost Per Mille (CPM) rates, such as finance, technology, and health.

Audience Retention: Improve audience retention to increase watch time and the likelihood of viewers encountering more ads.

Channel Memberships

Membership Perks: Offer exclusive perks to channel members who pay a monthly fee. This can include badges, emojis, members-only live chats, and exclusive content.

Creating Value: Ensure the perks are valuable and enticing to encourage viewers to join. Regularly update and add new perks to maintain interest.

Super Chat and Super Stickers

Live Streams: During live streams, viewers can purchase Super Chats and Super Stickers to highlight their messages and support your channel.

Engagement: Acknowledge and thank viewers who use Super Chat and Super Stickers to encourage more participation and generosity.

Merchandise Shelf

Merchandise Integration: Use YouTube's merchandise shelf to sell branded merchandise directly through your channel. Partner with services like Teespring or Spreadshop.

Design and Promotion: Create appealing and high-quality merchandise that resonates with your audience. Promote your merchandise in your videos and through social media.

Affiliate Marketing

Affiliate Programs: Join affiliate programs relevant to your niche. Promote products or services and earn a commission for each sale made through your unique affiliate links.

Amazon Associates: A popular choice for YouTubers, allowing you to earn commissions on a wide range of products.

Niche-Specific Programs: Look for affiliate programs related to your niche, such as tech gadgets, beauty products, or online courses.

Integration: Integrate affiliate links naturally into your content. Provide honest reviews, tutorials, and recommendations.

Transparency: Disclose affiliate links to maintain transparency and trust with your audience.

Sponsored Content and Brand Deals

Finding Sponsors: Reach out to brands relevant to your niche or use platforms like FameBit, Grapevine, or Social Bluebook to find sponsorship opportunities.

Negotiation: Negotiate fair compensation for sponsored content. Consider factors like video length, integration type, and audience reach.

Authenticity: Ensure sponsored content aligns with your brand and audience interests. Authenticity is crucial to maintaining viewer trust.

FTC Guidelines: Follow FTC guidelines by clearly disclosing sponsored content. Use phrases like "This video is sponsored by..." and include #ad or #sponsored in descriptions.

Crowdfunding and Donations

Patreon: Create a Patreon page where fans can support you with monthly contributions in exchange for exclusive perks and content.

Tiered Rewards: Offer tiered reward levels to cater to different budget ranges and provide increasing value.

Community Engagement: Engage with your patrons through exclusive content, polls, and direct interactions.

One-Time Donations: Use platforms like PayPal, Ko-fi, or Buy Me a Coffee to accept one-time donations from viewers who want to support your channel.

Creating and Selling Digital Products

E-Books and Guides: Write e-books or guides related to your niche and sell them through your website or platforms like Gumroad.

Online Courses: Develop and sell online courses on platforms like Udemy or Teachable. Share your expertise and provide in-depth learning experiences.

Digital Downloads: Offer digital downloads such as templates, presets, or artwork. These can be valuable resources for your audience.

Licensing Your Content

Content Licensing: License your videos or clips to media outlets, websites, or other creators. Use platforms like Jukin Media or Storyful to facilitate licensing deals.

Revenue Share: Earn a share of the revenue generated from your licensed content.

Building a Sustainable Income

Diversification: Diversify your income streams to create a sustainable and resilient business. Relying on multiple revenue sources reduces risk and ensures steady income.

Reinvestment: Reinvest a portion of your earnings back into your channel. Upgrade equipment, hire editors, or invest in marketing to enhance content quality and reach.

Long-Term Planning: Develop a long-term monetization strategy that aligns with your goals and values. Focus on creating value for your audience and building a lasting brand.

By implementing these monetization strategies, you can generate substantial revenue from your YouTube channel, turning your passion into a profitable business.

8

Leveraging Analytics and Insights

Leveraging Analytics and Insights

Understanding YouTube Analytics

Accessing Analytics: Use YouTube Studio to access detailed analytics about your channel's performance. Navigate to the Analytics tab for comprehensive data.

Key Metrics: Familiarize yourself with key metrics that provide insights into your channel's performance.

Views: Total number of views your videos receive.

Watch Time: Total minutes viewers spend watching your videos.

Average View Duration: Average time viewers spend on a single video.

Impressions: Number of times your video thumbnails were shown to viewers.

Click-Through Rate (CTR): Percentage of impressions that resulted in views.

Audience Retention: Percentage of your video that viewers watched.

Engagement: Likes, comments, shares, and other interactive elements.

Analyzing Audience Insight

Demographics: Understand the demographics of your audience, including age, gender, and geographic location. Tailor your content to better serve your primary audience.

Audience Behavior: Analyze viewer behavior to identify patterns and preferences.

Top Videos: Identify your most popular videos and understand what made them successful.

Traffic Sources: Determine where your viewers are coming from, such as search, suggested videos, or external websites.

Devices: See what devices your audience is using to watch your videos (e.g., mobile, desktop, tablet).

Optimizing Content with Data

Content Performance: Use analytics to evaluate which types of content perform best.

Trends: Identify trends in your successful videos, such as topics, formats, and lengths.

Retention Analysis: Analyze where viewers drop off in your videos to understand how to improve retention.

A/B Testing: Experiment with different video elements (titles, thumbnails, descriptions) to see which versions perform better.

Thumbnails: Test different thumbnail designs to see which attract more clicks.

Titles: Experiment with different titles to improve CTR and searchability.

Descriptions and Tags: Optimize descriptions and tags based on keyword performance.

Improving Viewer Engagements

Interactive Elements: Use end screens, cards, and calls to action to increase engagement.

End Screens: Promote other videos or playlists to keep viewers on your channel.

Cards: Insert cards at strategic points to link to related content or external websites.

Engagement Metrics: Focus on metrics that reflect viewer engagement.

Comments: Encourage viewers to leave comments and engage in discussions.

Likes/Dislikes: Monitor the like/dislike ratio to gauge audience satisfaction.

Shares: Track shares to understand how often and where your content is being shared.

Refining Your Content Strategies

Content Calendar: Develop a content calendar based on your analytics to plan and schedule videos strategically.

Frequency: Determine the optimal frequency for posting new videos based on audience engagement data.

Timing: Identify the best times to publish your videos when your audience is most active.

Content Mix: Balance different types of content (e.g., tutorials, vlogs, reviews) to keep your channel dynamic and appealing.

Trending Topics: Create content around trending topics in your niche to capitalize on current interests.

Evergreen Content: Produce evergreen content that remains relevant and continues to attract viewers over time.

Monitoring Competitors

Competitor Analysis: Study your competitors' channels to gain insights into their strategies and performance.

Content Strategy: Analyze their most popular videos and content themes.

Audience Engagement: Look at their engagement metrics to understand what resonates with their audience.

SEO Tactics: Examine their use of keywords, tags, and metadata to inform your own SEO strategies.

Benchmarking: Compare your channel's performance against your competitors to identify areas for improvement and opportunities for growth.

Adjusting Based on Feedback

Viewer Feedback: Pay close attention to viewer comments, messages, and social media interactions.

Addressing Concerns: Respond to constructive criticism and use it to improve your content.

Acknowledging Praise: Show appreciation for positive feedback and loyal viewers.

Surveys and Polls: Use surveys and polls to gather direct feedback from your audience.

Community Tab: Utilize the Community tab for polls and feedback questions.

Social Media: Conduct surveys on social media platforms to reach a broader audience.

Setting Goals and Measuring Success

SMART Goals: Set Specific, Measurable, Achievable, Relevant, and Time-bound goals for your channel.

Short-Term Goals: Focus on immediate objectives like improving video quality or increasing upload frequency.

Long-Term Goals: Plan for sustained growth, such as reaching specific subscriber milestones or expanding to new content formats.

Progress Tracking: Regularly review your analytics to track progress toward your goals.

Monthly Reviews: Conduct monthly performance reviews to assess progress and make necessary adjustments.

Annual Assessments: Evaluate your channel's performance annually to refine your long-term strategy.

Leveraging Advanced Tools

Third-Party Analytics Tools: Use advanced tools like TubeBuddy, VidIQ, or Social Blade for deeper insights and analytics.

Competitor Analysis: Gain detailed competitor insights and performance comparisons.

SEO Optimization: Get recommendations for optimizing your video metadata.

Custom Reports: Create custom reports to track specific metrics and trends relevant to your channel's goals.

By leveraging analytics and insights, you can make data-driven decisions to refine your content strategy, improve viewer engagement, and achieve sustained growth on your YouTube channel.

9

Building a Strong Brand Identity

Building a Strong Brand Identity

Defining Your Brand

Core Values and Mission: Clearly define your channel's core values and mission. Understand what you stand for and what message you want to convey to your audience.

Value Proposition: Identify what makes your channel unique and why viewers should subscribe.

Consistent Messaging: Ensure that your values and mission are reflected consistently across all your content and interactions.

Target Audience: Know your target audience inside and out. Understand their interests, preferences, and pain points.

Audience Personas: Create detailed personas representing different segments of your audience to guide your content creation and branding efforts.

Feedback and Engagement: Regularly seek feedback from your audience to stay aligned with their evolving needs and interests.

Visual Identity

Channel Art and Logo: Design professional and eye-catching channel art and a logo that reflect your brand's identity.

Banner: Your channel banner should include your logo, tagline, and a visual representation of your channel's theme.

Logo: Create a memorable logo that can be easily recognized across different platforms.

Thumbnails: Develop a consistent thumbnail style that makes your videos instantly recognizable.

Colors and Fonts: Use a consistent color palette and fonts that align with your brand identity.

Design Elements: Incorporate consistent design elements such as borders, logos, or watermarks.

Consistency: Maintain a cohesive visual style across all your videos and social media platforms.

Templates: Create templates for thumbnails, end screens, and social media posts to ensure visual consistency.

Style Guide: Develop a brand style guide outlining your visual identity guidelines.

Content Style and Tone

Voice and Tone: Establish a distinct voice and tone for your channel that resonates with your audience.

Personality: Infuse your personality into your content to create a genuine connection with viewers.

Language: Use language and terminology that align with your brand and audience preferences.

Content Formats: Develop signature content formats that viewers can associate with your channel.

Series and Segments: Create recurring series or segments to build anticipation and regular viewership.

Intro and Outro: Use consistent intros and outros to reinforce your brand identity and provide a professional touch.

Storytelling: Master the art of storytelling to engage viewers and make your content memorable.

Narrative Structure: Use a clear narrative structure with a beginning, middle, and end.

Emotional Connection: Evoke emotions and connect with viewers on a deeper level through compelling stories.

Branding Beyond YouTube

Social Media Presence: Extend your brand identity to social media platforms to reach a wider audience and enhance engagement.

Consistent Profiles: Use the same profile picture, banner, and bio across all social media accounts.

Cross-Promotion: Promote your YouTube content on social media and vice versa to drive traffic and build a cohesive brand presence.

Website and Blog: Create a dedicated website or blog to establish a central hub for your brand.

Content Hub: Use your website to host additional content, such as blog posts, resources, and exclusive videos.

Brand Store: Set up an online store to sell branded merchandise and digital products.

Email Marketing: Build an email list to maintain direct communication with your audience and promote your content.

Newsletters: Send regular newsletters with updates, behind-the-scenes content, and exclusive offers.

Lead Magnets: Offer valuable resources, such as e-books or guides, in exchange for email sign-ups.

Building Trust and Credibility

Transparency and Authenticity: Be transparent and authentic in all your interactions with your audience.

Behind-the-Scenes: Share behind-the-scenes content to give viewers a glimpse into your creative process.

Honesty: Be honest about sponsored content, product reviews, and any affiliations.

Consistency: Maintain a consistent upload schedule and content quality to build trust with your audience.

Scheduling: Use a content calendar to plan and stick to a consistent upload schedule.

Quality Control: Prioritize quality over quantity to ensure that every piece of content meets your brand's standards.

Engagement and Interaction: Actively engage with your audience to build a loyal community.

Responding to Comments: Regularly respond to comments and interact with viewers on social media.

Community Building: Foster a sense of community by acknowledging loyal viewers and creating opportunities for interaction.

Brand Partnerships and Collaborations

Strategic Partnerships: Form strategic partnerships with brands and creators that align with your brand values.

Brand Fit: Ensure that any brand partnerships are a natural fit for your channel and audience.

Collaborative Content: Create collaborative content that provides value to both your audience and your partner's audience.

Brand Ambassadorship: Position yourself as a brand ambassador for products or services you genuinely believe in.

Authentic Endorsements: Only endorse products or services that align with your values and that you can authentically support.

Long-Term Relationships: Build long-term relationships with brands for sustained collaboration and mutual growth.

Measuring Brand Impact

Brand Metrics: Track key metrics to measure the impact of your branding efforts.

Brand Awareness: Monitor metrics such as reach, impressions, and social media mentions.

Brand Loyalty: Track metrics like repeat viewership, subscriber growth, and audience retention.

Feedback and Perception: Regularly seek feedback from your audience to understand their perception of your brand.

Surveys and Polls: Use surveys and polls to gather direct feedback on your branding efforts.

Social Listening: Monitor social media conversations to gauge audience sentiment and perception.

By building a strong brand identity, you can differentiate your channel, foster viewer loyalty, and create a lasting impact in your niche.

10

Scaling and Sustaining Growth

Scaling and Sustaining Growth

Expanding Content Offering

Diversifying Content: Explore new content types and formats to keep your channel fresh and engaging.

Live Streams: Host live streams to interact with your audience in real-time and create a sense of community.

Shorts: Leverage YouTube Shorts to create bite-sized, engaging content that can attract new viewers.

Podcasts: Start a podcast to delve deeper into topics and provide valuable content in an audio format.

Guest Appearances: Invite guests from your niche or industry to appear in your videos, adding variety and fresh perspectives.

User-Generated Content: Encourage your audience to create and submit content, fostering a sense of community and engagement.

Leveraging Cross-Platform Promotion

Social Media Marketing: Utilize social media platforms to promote your content and engage with your audience.

Consistent Posting: Regularly share updates, teasers, and behind-the-scenes content on platforms like Instagram, Twitter, and Facebook.

Hashtags and Trends: Use relevant hashtags and participate in trending topics to increase visibility.

Collaborations Beyond YouTube: Collaborate with influencers and creators on other platforms to reach new audiences.

Instagram Takeovers: Participate in Instagram takeovers with other influencers to cross-promote each other's content.

TikTok Challenges: Create or join TikTok challenges to tap into a wider audience.

Email Marketing: Maintain regular communication with your subscribers through newsletters and updates.

Exclusive Content: Offer exclusive content, such as early access to videos or special insights, to email subscribers.

Investing in Quality and Professionalism

Upgrading Equipment: Continuously invest in high-quality equipment to improve your production value.

Cameras and Lighting: Upgrade to better cameras and lighting setups to enhance video quality.

Audio Equipment: Invest in high-quality microphones and audio equipment for clearer sound.

Professional Editing: Consider hiring professional editors or using advanced editing software to polish your videos.

Visual Effects: Incorporate visual effects and graphics to make your videos more engaging.

Music and Sound Effects: Use royalty-free music and sound effects to enhance your videos' appeal.

Team Expansion: As your channel grows, consider building a team to help manage different aspects of your channel.

Content Creators: Collaborate with other content creators to produce more varied and frequent content.

Social Media Managers: Hire social media managers to maintain a consistent and engaging online presence.

Marketing Experts: Work with marketing experts to develop and execute growth strategies.

Engaging with Your Community

Building a Community: Foster a sense of community among your viewers to increase loyalty and engagement.

Community Tab: Use the Community tab on YouTube to post updates, polls, and interact with your audience.

Exclusive Groups: Create exclusive groups or forums for your most loyal viewers to engage more deeply.

Feedback and Interaction: Actively seek and respond to viewer feedback to show that you value their input.

Q&A Sessions: Host regular Q&A sessions to address viewer questions and build a closer connection.

Feedback Forms: Use feedback forms or surveys to gather insights and suggestions from your audience.

Fan Engagement: Recognize and reward your most engaged fans to foster loyalty.

Fan Features: Feature fan art, comments, or content in your videos to show appreciation.

Giveaways: Host giveaways and contests to reward loyal viewers and encourage participation.

Monetization and Financial Growth

Diversified Revenue Streams: Develop multiple revenue streams to ensure financial stability and growth.

Ad Revenue: Continue to optimize ad revenue through YouTube Partner Program.

Sponsorships: Secure sponsorships and brand deals to add a reliable income source.

Merchandise: Expand your merchandise offerings to cater to different segments of your audience.

Online Courses: Create and sell online courses or workshops related to your niche.

Financial Management: Implement sound financial management practices to sustain and grow your income.

Budgeting: Create and stick to a budget to manage your expenses and investments.

Savings and Investments: Save a portion of your income and consider investing in growth opportunities.

Scaling Operations: Efficiently scale your operations to handle increased demand and content production.

Automation: Use automation tools to streamline repetitive tasks such as scheduling and posting.

Outsourcing: Outsource tasks like editing, marketing, and administrative work to focus on content creation.

Staying Ahead of Trends

Industry Trends: Stay updated on the latest trends and changes in the YouTube ecosystem.

Algorithm Updates: Keep track of YouTube algorithm updates and adjust your strategies accordingly.

Content Trends: Monitor trending topics and formats within your niche to stay relevant.

Innovative Content: Experiment with new content ideas and formats to keep your channel fresh and engaging.

Summary

"How to Get Millions of Subscribers on YouTube" is a comprehensive guide that unveils the essential strategies and insider secrets needed to achieve remarkable success on the platform. From mastering YouTube SEO and creating engaging content to building a strong brand identity and monetizing your channel effectively, this book equips aspiring YouTubers with the tools to attract and retain millions of subscribers. Packed with actionable advice, real-world examples, and practical tips, this guide is a road map for navigating the complexities of YouTube, fostering audience loyalty, and ultimately turning creative passion into sustainable growth and financial reward.

All Rights Reserved
Fredrick Wonders
2024

www.ingramcontent.com/pod-product-compliance
Lightning Source LLC
Chambersburg PA
CBHW071948210526
45479CB00003B/858